GREAT WAR LITERATURE

NOTES

Written by W Lawrance

on

THE RETURN OF THE SOLDIER

A NOVEL BY REBECCA WEST

Great War Literature Notes on The Return of the Soldier, a novel by Rebecca West
Written by W Lawrance

Published by:
Great War Literature Publishing LLP
Forum House, Stirling Road, Chichester, PO19 7DN
Web site: *www.greatwarliterature.co.uk*
E-Mail: *admin@greatwarliterature.co.uk*

Produced in Great Britain

First Published 2005.
This Edition published 2014. Copyright ©2005-2014 Wendy Lawrance.
The moral right of the author has been asserted.

ISBN 978-1910603062 Paperback Edition 2
Replaces earlier edition: 978-1905378357

10 9 8 7 6 5 4 3 2 1

Design and production by Great War Literature Publishing LLP
Typeset in Neue Helvetica, ITC Berkeley Old Style and Trajan Pro

Great War Literature Notes on

The Return of the Soldier

CONTENTS

PREFACE

The primary purpose of Great War Literature Study Guides is to provide in-depth analysis of First World War literature for GCSE and A-Level students.

Great War Literature Publishing have taken the positive decision to produce a uniquely detailed and in-depth interpretation of selected works for students. We also actively promote the publication of our works in an electronic format via the Internet to give the broadest possible access.

Our publications can be used in isolation or in collaboration with other study guides. It is our aim to provide assistance with your understanding of First World War literature, not to provide the answers to specific questions. This approach provides the resources that allow the student the freedom to reach their own conclusions and express an independent viewpoint.

The structure of Great War Literature Study Guides allows the reader to delve into a required section easily without the need to read from beginning to end.

The Great War Literature Study Guides have been thoroughly researched and are the result of over 30 years of experience of studying this particular genre.

Studying literature is not about being right or wrong, it is entirely a matter of opinion. The secret to success is developing the ability to form these opinions and to deliver them succinctly and reinforce them with quotes and clear references from the text.

Great War Literature Study Guides help to extend your knowledge of First World War literature and offer clear definitions and guidance to enhance your studying. Our clear and simple layouts make the guides easy to access and understand.

The Great War Literature Study Guide on *The Return of the Soldier*, provides a critical assessment of many aspects of this novel and is based entirely on the opinion of the author of this guide.

INTRODUCTION

The Return of the Soldier is a story of moral courage, of changing times, of social attitudes and of love. Recounting the effects of the war on a select group of people, this book has very little reference to trench-life and, as such, could be classified as a home-front novel - showing how the war and its after-effects would change forever the lives of those who had lived through it.

Set in the spring of 1916, this story is narrated by Jenny, the adoring cousin of 'the soldier', Chris Baldry who, having undergone some unnamed trauma, is now suffering from amnesia. Chris has forgotten his wife Kitty and their life at his family home, Baldry Court and believes that he is still in love with Margaret, with whom he had a brief relationship fifteen years earlier. These three women, brought together by their concern for Chris, face a dilemma: if they leave Chris as he is, he will be safe from the war; if they 'cure' him, he will have to go back. Whatever they decide, they all realise that someone must lose, the question is: who should that be?

In making this difficult decision, the women learn a great deal about each other and themselves, as well as seeing a side of Chris which, for Jenny and Kitty, is surprising and unexpected. Each of the women have their own motives and concerns but they must decide whether it is better for this mentally damaged man to live a lie but be safe and happy, or become, once again, what he was before: the soldier.

THE RETURN OF THE SOLDIER
BY REBECCA WEST

SYNOPSIS

CHAPTER ONE

The story opens with Kitty and Jenny sitting in the nursery of Baldry Court. We immediately learn that the child who should have inhabited this room is now dead. There are no other children in the house, although this room has been preserved as it was when the child was alive. Jenny remembers happier times when the child, Oliver, had played in this room. Kitty reveals that she always comes to the nursery to dry her hair because of the bright sunshine that floods the room. While she pushes a chair towards the window, Kitty admits to Jenny that she would have preferred that this room had not been preserved by her husband, Chris, especially as, she implies, there will be no more children.

Kitty sits in the window while Jenny brushes her hair. Jenny looks out of the window at the beautifully manicured lawns below. Her thoughts readily turn to her cousin, Chris, who is away at the front. Jenny longs for his safe return, particularly as, of late, she has been having nightmares about him. She speaks of her desire to hear from Chris, but is admonished by Kitty whose assurance of her husband's safety seems firm. Kitty is convinced that, if anything was wrong, she would have been informed. Jenny begins to ponder her surroundings - Kitty has a talent for creating beauty and Jenny feels proud that, in Chris's absence, they have managed to preserve - and even enhance - his beloved Baldry Court.

Jenny also remembers Chris's final morning before he departed for France. She recalls how he had visited the rooms and grounds before taking one final longing look at the exterior. Jenny interprets this as an acknowledgement of his contentment with his life and surroundings. She remembers how happy he had been. When she voices this opinion, Kitty is quick to agree with her.

In the silence that follows, Jenny recollects her childhood and times spent with Chris: his vivid, playful imagination and longing for an adventurous life. This wish had been stifled by the death of his father when Chris had taken over the family business and responsibilities. His marriage to Kitty had been a further financial burden, but all of this was easy compared to the death of his son. Jenny realises that keeping Chris happy has become the object of her existence: in his absence, her life seems empty.

The parlourmaid enters with a card from a Mrs William Grey who has called to see Kitty. This woman has come from Wealdstone, which is only three miles away, but it would seem is a much less fashionable area. Mrs Grey, although unknown to both Kitty and Jenny, has called to bring them news. Kitty decides that she will see Mrs Grey, while commenting on the lack of refinement in her address. This sense of superiority is exacerbated by the visitor's appearance. Jenny mentally notes Mrs Grey's shabby clothes and care-worn features as she and Kitty descend the stairs to greet her.

After a short while, Mrs Grey reveals her news: she has been notified that Captain Baldry is wounded. Kitty and Jenny both receive this news with incredulity: they believe that Mrs Grey must be attempting to deceive them. If this news was true, Kitty would have been informed by the War Office. Jenny, whose feelings for Mrs Grey are more of pity than anger, tries to remain detached from this situation. Kitty, however, fancying that she is about to entrap Mrs Grey as an imposter, seems to be almost enjoying questioning their visitor. Mrs Grey attempts to explain that Chris is not, in fact, physically wounded, but is suffering from shell-shock. Kitty continues with her probing questions, many of which Mrs Grey struggles to answer satisfactorily.

Jenny, feeling uncomfortable, begins to wish for an end to this scene, when suddenly, and for the first time, Mrs Grey refers to Chris by his first name. Kitty is angry at this familiarity and openly accuses Mrs Grey of fraud, telling her to leave. Jenny is embarrassed by Kitty's outburst and asks Mrs Grey to give them more details.

Mrs Grey explains that she had known Chris fifteen years earlier - she describes him as a family friend. She is now a married women and had felt it only fair to inform Chris's wife of his predicament. She produces a telegram and explains that Chris seems to have lost his memory. The telegram had been addressed to her as Margaret Allington which was her maiden name.

Even when she has read the telegram, Kitty still refuses to believe Margaret. There has also been a letter from Chris, but Margaret will not allow Kitty to see this. She appears defensive, repeating that she has not seen Chris for fifteen years. Finally, she leaves and Jenny and Kitty discuss the consequences of her visit. We learn that the content of the telegram had revealed a closer relationship than Margaret Grey had admitted: Chris had called her by a nickname. Kitty assumes that this either means Chris is mad - a situation she believes is too awful to contemplate; or else that he has been keeping some dreadful secret from her. She is hurt at the discovery of another woman in her husband's life. Jenny, on the other hand, merely focuses on the fact that Chris needs help.

CHAPTER TWO

The day after Margaret's visit, Jenny receives a letter from another cousin, Frank Baldry. Frank is in Boulogne, where he has been visiting Chris, who had sent a telegram requesting that his cousin visit him. Frank explains that Chris had sent this telegram to a parish in which he had been curate fifteen years ago. He also expresses his surprise at not seeing Kitty and Jenny on the boat to France. In his letter, he explains the curious nature of his visit and Chris's unfolding story.

During Frank's visit, it would seem that Chris had explained his feelings for a young woman named Margaret. Unaware of his cousin's amnesia, Frank had initially assumed that Chris and Margaret were having an affair, and had been for over fifteen years. Chris had asked Frank to fetch Margaret from England and expressed his desire to marry her. Appalled at this suggestion, Frank had pointed out that Chris was already married - to Kitty. Chris had seemed unaware of Kitty's existence, which made Frank realise that Chris had lost his memory.

Frank had set about explaining that Chris had been married for ten years and that his father had died twelve years ago. This whole episode had been very upsetting for Chris, whose longing for Margaret seemed to overshadow everything. This episode revealed a side of Chris which Frank had never seen before and he had been shocked by his cousin's passionate reactions. The doctors had then advised Frank that Chris should be taken home and his letter ends with him saying that he intends to bring his cousin back to Baldry Court the following week.

On the day of Chris's arrival, Kitty and Jenny are filled with anticipation and foreboding. For Kitty, this takes the form of finding fault with everything and everyone in the house. Jenny just seems distracted. When he eventually arrives, Jenny notices how much he seems to have aged, although he has only been away for a year. Despite her joy at seeing him, Jenny's reactions are tempered by the knowledge that she no longer appears as he would remember her. Of Kitty, however, he obviously has no recollection whatsoever. His attitude to his wife is faltering and uncertain which means that she is obliged to introduce herself to him and the atmosphere becomes very formal. Chris notices the changes in the house - all of which he had been aware of before his departure for France - but which now seem strange.

Chris and Kitty go to dress for dinner and when Kitty returns, Jenny notices that she has changed into a white dress, reminiscent of the one she had worn on her wedding day. She has made herself look virginal and innocent. Chris's entrance is less composed: he falls down the stairs because had has forgotten that they have been changed. However, the sight of Kitty, sitting serenely, captivates him. This is a transient emotion, however: despite Kitty's beauty, his thoughts seem always distant - he is remembering Margaret and is constantly aware of the strangeness of his surroundings. Again, an awkward silence descends.

During dinner, Chris seems to be in a reflective mood. He appears to feel trapped in an unfamiliar house, surrounded by strangers, yet trying to behave as though everything is normal. Kitty tries, vainly, to remind him of their lives and obligations, but Chris merely seems confused and careworn. He points out, very politely and apologetically, that he must see Margaret - he feels as though his life depends on meeting her again. Kitty agrees to this request and says that Margaret will be brought to see him the next day. Despite this outward appearance of kindness and generosity, once Chris has left the room, Kitty shows how she really feels: she is angry and disappointed. She believes that Chris is having an affair with Margaret and is merely pretending that he has lost his memory. Jenny reacts violently towards Kitty, shaking her by the shoulders. Chris witnesses this and begs them to at least try to be civil to each other. Kitty responds like a petulant child and storms off to her bedroom, leaving Chris and Jenny alone.

After a short silence, they begin to talk. Chris reveals that he does remember Kitty, but only as a *type* of woman - not specifically as his wife. Jenny defends Kitty and tries to help Chris to understand what has happened. It becomes clear, however, that to Chris, the only memories he has, or wants, are of Margaret, her home at Monkey Island, and a warm spring fifteen years earlier. He decides to tell Jenny about his memories...

CHAPTER THREE

Chris's Story...

Chris describes Monkey Island and the inn which Margaret's father had owned. That spring, while staying with his Uncle Ambrose, he had visited Margaret and her father. He describes Margaret with clarity and affection and makes no secret of his deep love for her. He does not speak of their final day together, or their parting, as it would seem that the last thing he can remember is another, happier day. On this occasion, Mr Allington had been away from home and Uncle Ambrose had gone to town which meant that Chris and Margaret had been alone all afternoon. They had walked and talked and served tea to customers at the inn. Later, in the dark, Chris had spoken to Margaret of his love for her - the type of love which nothing can alter.

As he finishes this story, Jenny notices a change in Chris, as he comes back to the reality of his life now. She seems to understand his need for Margaret - this is a side of Chris which she has never seen before and she is pleased and proud that he felt able to share it with her.

CHAPTER FOUR

It is the next day and Jenny must go to Wealdstone to fetch Margaret. Before she leaves, Jenny goes out into the garden, where she finds Chris rowing on the pond. She tells him of her mission and, in a moment of compassion, wanting to brace him for the physical changes he will see in his beloved, she reveals that Margaret has already visited the house and that she is aged, worn and married. Chris does not seem to care. He reiterates that theirs was a love which transcends change and cannot be touched by something so minor as altered appearances.

So Jenny goes to Wealdstone and finds Margaret's house. Margaret seems to sense that Jenny's visit indicates that Chris has come home. She is apologetic about her appearance, but invites Jenny in, eager to learn about Chris. Unable to look at Margaret, Jenny reveals the depth of her cousin's feelings and his desire to meet Margaret again. On hearing all of this, Margaret is moved to tears and Jenny finds herself feeling unexpectedly sympathetic towards this drab, homely woman. Despite her misgivings, Margaret also wants to see Chris, yet she is worried that to do so will hurt Kitty. Jenny assuages this guilt by pointing out that she is there at Kitty's request. Margaret seems gratified and praises Kitty's kindness. All at once, Jenny sees Margaret in a different light - she no longer seems old and dreary, but beautiful and joyous.

This dream-like state is shattered by the entrance of Mr Grey - Margaret's husband - who had been out in the garden. Margaret joins him in the kitchen and explains that she is going to visit an old friend who has been injured, but that she will leave him with enough food prepared for his tea. He accepts this and goes back to the garden. When Margaret returns to the parlour, she is ready to leave. Jenny seems worried that Margaret is bound to have changed so much during the past fifteen years, but she continues on her mission to bring Margaret and Chris together and they begin their journey to Baldry Court.

Margaret seems to feel uneasy in such a grand car, so Jenny encourages her to talk about Chris. She is intrigued to know why they parted. Margaret tells a similar story to the one Chris had told the night before and her love for him is at once apparent. Jenny, however, presses her for information about their parting and Margaret seems happy to reveal her story…

A week had passed since Chris had declared his love for her and they had spent that time together, enjoying the secrecy of their feelings. Then, one afternoon, Margaret had gone rowing with Bert, the nephew of another innkeeper and an old family friend. Chris had arrived and witnessed them larking about on the river. He had come over, it would seem, to say goodbye to Margaret because he had to go away that evening. He was extremely angry at finding her enjoying the company of another man. Despite Margaret's protestations of innocence, an angry row had erupted between them, and they parted on bad terms.

This account of their parting reveals much to Jenny, for now she can remember that particular spring and Chris's prolonged absence from Baldry Court. She recalls that there had been some trouble connected with the family business and that Chris had been summoned home by his anxious father. Jenny remembers his arrival home and how lost he had looked: not really seeing anything. The very next day he had departed for Mexico to sort out business matters and save the family honour. That day had marked the end of his youth. While Jenny is assimilating this information, Margaret continues with her story…

Three days after her argument with Chris, Margaret's father had died and she had been forced to sell the inn and go into service as a mother's help. She had met Mr Grey, who was the brother-in-law of one of the mothers with whom she had found employment. They were married five years after her parting from Chris, from whom she had heard nothing since the day he left.

Margaret had not returned to Monkey Island, partly because Mr Grey's health had, for many years, been poor. Also she had worried that the place might no longer be the paradise of her memories. However, finding herself greatly distressed by some unspoken event in her life, Margaret and her husband had visited the Island. They found the inn, beautifully kept and were welcomed by the owners, Mr Taylor and his daughter. They had stayed for lunch and afterwards, Mr Taylor, having learned that Margaret used to live at the inn, had contrived to spend some time alone with her. He had sat her down and handed her twelve letters which Chris had sent. Mr Taylor had discovered these when he bought the inn. Out of loyalty to her husband, Margaret had not read these letters. They had remained unopened until she received the telegram from Chris, but now she seems to regret that their existence and contents had remained a secret for so many years.

They arrive at Baldry Court and Margaret comments on its size and the amount of work which Chris must have had to do in order to maintain it. She seems to have a great understanding of Chris's nature, which surprises Jenny, although she still finds it difficult to warm to this stranger. Margaret feels and looks out of place in the grand house which Kitty has fashioned. Jenny orders tea and while they drink it, Jenny imagines how Chris will react to the alteration in this woman who he remembers as a girl. Margaret, however, is keen to see Chris and Jenny points out where he can be found, before watching her cross the lawn in the direction of the pond.

Jenny goes upstairs, tinged with jealousy towards Margaret. She consoles herself slightly, with the knowledge that she is surrounded by a beauty that *will* last - Baldry Court. She finds Kitty sitting at the window of the nursery, and suddenly realises that she feels more sympathy for Margaret than she does for Kitty. Together they look at the scene outside the window. Chris runs towards Margaret, before falling to his knees before her. She helps him to his feet and Jenny finds that she can no longer bear to look. She fears that his quite understandable rejection of Margaret's aged appearance will be too much for their visitor to bear. When she eventually plucks up the courage to look again, she finds them gazing affectionately at one another as though there had been no passage of time. The couple turn and walk into the woods. Kitty, who has also witnessed this scene, weeps openly, while Jenny reflects silently on the strength of true love.

CHAPTER FIVE

Later, when Margaret has left, Chris speaks to Kitty, saying that Margaret has helped him to understand his situation. He means this kindly, but Kitty reacts angrily - he should have believed *her*, rather than seeking confirmation from another woman. Chris is stung by this rebuke, but at least Kitty seems now to have accepted that his amnesia is genuine.

Margaret continues to visit often and Jenny notices that it is only in her presence that Chris seems to come alive. He treasures even the smallest gift from her, while barely noticing the beautiful objects with which Kitty has filled the house. Kitty wallows in self-pity and apathy, while Jenny tries desperately to detach herself from these events, so that she does not have to think about them. In their own way, they are grieving.

A week later, Kitty has arranged for Dr Gilbert Anderson to visit. She sees him as her best chance of getting Chris back to normal. While walking, Jenny realises that she longs for the company of Chris and Margaret as she feels an affinity with them that she cannot feel for Kitty. Suddenly she is overcome with jealousy - their shared affection and experiences make her realise that she has lost Chris forever. She feels as though his decision to live in the past proves his rejection of the present - and her. In turning from Kitty (the embodiment of outward beauty) to Margaret (a representative of earthly goodness), Chris has revealed a side of his personality which seems incongruous in Kitty's perfectly created surroundings. At that moment, Jenny longs for the doctor to 'cure' Chris, to bring him back into her world - the world she used to share with him.

She goes to find Chris and Margaret, to tell them of the doctor's impending visit and that their presence at the house is required. She finds them in a clearing in the wood: Chris is sleeping on a rug, while Margaret sits at his side, watching him. Margaret's desire to protect him is the thought which first comes to Jenny. She sees that *she* had been able to do nothing for Chris, whereas this woman, simply by loving him, has brought comfort and purpose to his confused world. Jenny, at last, appreciates that all the while he continues to live in the past, the army will not take him back - he will be safe and they have Margaret to thank for that. Although, when Chris wakes up, Jenny feels duty-bound to tell them about the doctor's visit, she knows this will have no impact on them. They will see him, of course, but nothing can come between them.

CHAPTER SIX

They all return to the house and Jenny becomes more apprehensive about the doctor's visit. They find Dr Anderson outside the entrance to the house. He dismisses the two women and takes Chris for a walk in the garden, where they can talk privately. Jenny and Margaret wait in the hall for the Doctor and Chris to return. They are soon joined by Kitty who bids Margaret to go upstairs and remove her coat. Initially, Margaret politely refuses, but Jenny persuades her that this would be for the best, and goes with her. In the privacy of Jenny's room, Margaret discloses her admiration of Kitty's beauty. While re-arranging her hair, Margaret expresses her concerns for Chris, and Jenny is touched by the depth of her love for him, and her goodness, which seems no less than Chris deserves. All of a sudden, Margaret cries out - she has seen a photograph of Oliver - Chris and Kitty's son. Jenny explains that Oliver has been dead for five years, whereupon Margaret reveals that she too had a son, who also died five years ago, at the same age as Oliver. Margaret collapses to the floor, momentarily overwhelmed with grief for the loss of these two infants.

This scene is interrupted by the parlourmaid, announcing that Mrs Baldry and the doctor are waiting downstairs. With a sense of foreboding, Jenny and Margaret go down to the drawing room. The doctor confirms that Chris's amnesia is genuine - he explains that no amount of self-discipline can bring Chris back to reality. There is, he says, some unspoken, subconcious unhappiness which has caused Chris to block out the past fifteen years of his life. Dr Anderson tries to discover why Chris might have done this - what had been missing from his life? Kitty exclaims that Chris was happy with her, but this is refuted by the doctor: Chris *must* have been deeply unhappy with his life when he joined the army as he consciously chose not to register his home address or Kitty's name with the War Office. Kitty, in desperation, tries to blame this 'oversight' on his forgetfulness, but again the doctor denies that Chris could have done this without being aware of the implications. Kitty points out, with some bitterness, that when Chris had been hypnotised, he was capable of remembering his old life. The doctor dismisses this as irrelevant in this case - he needs to know from Kitty what it was that had made Chris unhappy before he left.

By now, Kitty is beginning to lose her temper, so the doctor placates her by pointing out that she is not to blame. Dr Anderson now turns his attentions to Jenny, who suggests that her cousin may have always felt a long-standing dissatisfaction with his life. When the doctor poses a question regarding Chris's attitude to sex, Margaret shyly breaks the embarrassed silence by pointing out that she had always found him vulnerable in such matters. This knowledge shocks Jenny, who had always thought of Chris as strong and magnificent.

Margaret boldly takes over the conversation and suggests that there can be no 'cure' for Chris: by bringing him back to reality, the doctor will simply be making him less happy, and more ordinary. Dr Anderson agrees with her, but still sees it as his duty to discover a means of bringing Chris back, whereupon Margaret points out that if they remind him of his dead son, his memory might return. The doctor had been unaware of Oliver's existence, but thinks this may be the key to Chris's unhappiness. Margaret suggests that they show him something which had belonged to the boy. The doctor says that Margaret will have to be the one to do this - to bring his two worlds together. Kitty heartily agrees, although Jenny, Margaret and the doctor all seem unsure that this is the wisest course, or that there is any need to rush matters. However, Kitty is adamant, so Jenny and Margaret are sent to the nursery to find some suitable reminder.

Once there, they talk about Oliver and Margaret's dead son, Dick, while Jenny searches through drawers and cupboards for something that might remind Chris of his son. Margaret becomes despondent at the thought of the two dead infants, but Jenny eventually finds the items she was looking for: a sweater and a ball. Having inspected them and held them, Margaret gives them back and tells Jenny to put them away again - she cannot show them to Chris. Jenny is pleased - this could be his salvation. After all, she reasons, Chris is happy and he is safe, so why should that be taken away from him?

Suddenly, Margaret notices Kitty standing in the doorway, cradling her neglected dog and crying. Jenny sees that in allowing Chris to remain happy and oblivious, they will be denying him the truth and that, she realises, is just as important as happiness. He cannot be allowed to grow old, believing himself to be twenty-one years of age and in the first flush of young love - it would be demeaning and dishonest. He would, she thinks, become an object of fun.

Margaret has obviously realised this too, as she now picks up the ball and sweater and reluctantly goes outside to find Chris. Initially Jenny tries to find solace in the thought that she might be able to help Chris to feel happy again. Then she is joined in the nursery by Kitty, who is impatient for the whole situation to be resolved. She instructs Jenny to look out of the window and report on what she can see. She wants to know if Chris is coming back to the house yet. To start with, Jenny sees nothing, but when she looks again, a few minutes later, she sees Chris and Margaret embrace before he turns and walks towards the house. He has the bearing of a soldier and a forced smile.

Jenny describes his soldierly appearance to a desperate Kitty, who quietly creeps over to the window to see for herself. She alone rejoices that Chris is back to normal: he has been cured; he has returned to her.

CHARACTER ANALYSIS

1. CHRIS

In reality, Chris is a thirty-six year old Captain, who has become a victim of shell-shock while serving at the front, and as a result, has lost his memory. He believes himself to be twenty-one and still in love with Margaret Allington, whereas he is in fact married to Kitty and they live, with his cousin Jenny, at his family home, Baldry Court at Harrow-Weald.

During the course of the novel, we learn about his two different personalities. It is through Jenny, the narrator of the story, that we, like her, make these discoveries. Jenny has always believed Chris to be a strong, self-controlled and responsible man; hard-working and with definite ideas about the people and things in his life. He had always seemed to believe that women should be beautiful, demure and dispassionate.

Chris had been forced to take on great responsibilities when his father died. The running of the family home and business had become his burden, which only increased following his marriage to Kitty. The death of their infant son had caused him great unhappiness, but as Jenny and Kitty were doing their utmost to keep him contented, it would seem he had managed to continue with this existence, which is always described with an air of false contentment. His surroundings were perfectly maintained, his life was ordered and refined.

The Chris who returns to Baldry Court is compliant, kind and polite. He has no conscious intention of wounding Kitty and he tries to shield her from his real feelings. This proves impossible and he is forced to beg to be allowed to see Margaret. he is sensible of the impropriety of this request, but his desire for Margaret is consuming and overwhelming him. Seeing Margaret again seems to bring him back to life: with her he is happy, yet when she is absent, he is withdrawn and reclusive.

During her conversations with Chris and Margaret, Jenny learns of a different side of his personality. When Margaret had known him, he was less refined and more open and emotional, although still slightly haughty. During one spring with Margaret, he had experienced more joy and fulfillment than in a lifetime at Baldry Court. When she first sees his home, Margaret expresses her concern about the amount of time and effort he must have had to put into maintaining the building and lifestyle. This surprises Jenny until she realises that Baldry Court and their existence there is a pretence, maintained because that is what she and Kitty had believed Chris wanted. Margaret's comment reveals the reality: Chris's idea of a truly splendid house, would have been a home, built with hearts, rather than hands. He would have wanted to build and share a life, a home and a family - not have it all done perfectly for him, while he merely provided the funds to allow such a lifestyle.

When Chris speaks of his unerring love for Margaret, he reveals a passionate and deep capacity to feel, of which Jenny seems to have been unaware. He does not care whether she has aged and withered - in his mind she will always be as he remembers her. Jenny learns, through Chris, that real, lasting love is not about appearances: in order to survive, it has to be deeper than that.

Chris does not seem to remember his parting from Margaret, but she reveals the truth: a petty argument resulting from his jealousy. This demonstrates several aspects of Chris: he presumably felt ashamed of his actions and he has forgotten that day and consigned it to his catalogue of unhappy thoughts; he was initially stubborn, but then contrite - he wrote twelve letters to Margaret, despite receiving no response from her. The constancy of his love is shown by this action.

The interview between the three women and Dr Anderson is also very revealing. The doctor states a fact which should have been obvious to them from the beginning: Chris cannot have been truly happy before he went to the war, otherwise he would not have neglected to give his correct address and contact details to the War Office. This demonstrates his deep sadness and subconsciously it is possible that he was trying to escape from his life at Baldry Court. This was a decision which he had made in full awareness of the possible far-reaching consequences - Kitty might never have known what had happened to him. He had taken leave of Baldry Court in a manner which implied finality and suggested that he did not intend to return. This could mean that he expected to die during the War, or that he anticipated a new life afterwards.

Once he is made aware of it, the doctor seems to believe that it was Oliver's death that was the cause of Chris's unhappiness. The fact that reminding him of his son successfully returns Chris's memory could be said to reinforce this. However, it is not clear that he had ever been as happy with Kitty as he was with Margaret. Kitty and Jenny had contrived to make him comfortable, but they did not really know him, or understand his feelings. That was an intimacy which he had only shared with Margaret.

This rediscovered joy is snatched from him and in returning to his soldierly status, we get a glimpse of his old personality. As he walks across the lawn, his appearance has changed: he has lost his carefree spirit and become stiff and withdrawn again. He does not appear to look forward to greeting Kitty: he does not run to her and fall at *her* feet as he had done to Margaret. One can sense his reserve and propriety have returned: as has his sadness.

2. KITTY

Of all the characters involved in this novel, Kitty is the one with whom the reader most expects to sympathise. However, her personality and reactions make this impossible. Throughout the story, her initially poised and beautiful countenance seems to disintegrate, as she reveals that her appearance is a façade behind which lies a vain, selfish woman with a callous disregard for everyone else.

Kitty gives the impression of being a fairly one-dimensional character, whose relatively happy and comfortable existence is shattered by her husband's amnesia. Interestingly it would seem that this occurrence has caused a greater disturbance to Kitty than his absence. At the beginning of the story, she is portrayed as a dutiful wife, continuing with her life, unflustered by the fact that Chris has not written to her for two weeks. She seems to be a calm woman of great self-possession and dignity.

Kitty and Chris have obviously reacted differently to Oliver's death. The child has been dead for five years, yet we learn that, against Kitty's will, Chris has had the nursery preserved as though he were still alive. It would appear that Chris wants to remember his son, while Kitty is desperate to put this unhappy time behind her. She hints that there will be no more children for her and Chris and, although this may be due to some unspoken medical problem, it could also provide a hint that their relationship is far from happy.

She greets the initial news of Chris's illness with contempt and disbelief and, even when Jenny says that she believes it must be true, Kitty still seems doubtful: as though she cannot accept that anything bad should be allowed to intrude upon her perfectly maintained world. Upon receiving confirmation from Frank that Chris really is ill, Kitty's first reaction is that of a sulky child, disappointed at her husband's dislike of her singing. Suddenly, however, she panics and begs Jenny to make sure Chris is brought home. Maybe she senses that his continued amnesia endangers her way of life and hopes that, by having him at home, his memory may more easily return.

Initially, when he does come home, Kitty appears nervous, but when Chris seems unsure of how to behave towards her, she becomes child-like once again. Later, she adopts a more obvious means of reminding him of his past: she chooses a dress in a style similar to that of her bridal gown. This ploy fails - although Chris appreciates her beauty, it fails to really touch him. She continues, during that first evening, to try to remind him of his past - not necessarily with words, but with her actions. All of this is to no avail - he wants Margaret, not her. She appears to take his rejection quite well, but inwardly she is seething with rage, which she expresses only when Chris has left the room. Her reactions suggest that appearances are more important to her than anything else: she is not concerned for Chris, but believes that his amnesia must be an excuse for having an affair with Margaret. Everything in her life is looked upon only as it relates to her - she will have to tolerate this situation, as other women do. She seems more upset that Chris would choose to have an affair with an unattractive woman, than that he might have been unfaithful in the first place. Her vanity and snobbery show here, as she attributes his choice to a desire for change - he has always been surrounded by beauty, so the dowdy, lower-class Margaret obviously provides some relief for him. When Jenny reacts violently to this assertion, Kitty becomes petulant and throws a tantrum.

When Margaret visits Chris for the first time, Kitty does not acknowledge her presence, but sits in the nursery, staring out of the window. She seems to be clinging on to her old way of life by sitting there where she feels a connection with Chris and their past. When Margaret has gone she shows Chris her anger for the first time, although this also marks her reluctant acceptance that Chris is not pretending and the beginning of her detached self-pity.

Kitty's main concern is that Chris should be 'cured', that he should return to her and that her life should be as it was before. The doctor, Jenny and Margaret all harbour reservations about this course of action, but to Kitty, this is clear: she must have Chris back - her life will not be ruined by his illness. She seems blissfully unaware that by 'curing' him, he will not physically return to her because he will have to go back to the front, where he may be killed. This demonstrates her selfish nature. It is not his welfare or safety that concerns her, but that her life should not be affected by anything that has happened to him.

Eventually, of course, Kitty gets her own way: but one has the impression that she always does. The reader should feel happy for her - her husband has returned. Yet such a feeling is impossible. In trying so desperately to cling on to her supposedly perfect world, she has cruelly destroyed his dreams and his future.

3. JENNY

Jenny, as the narrator of the story, is able to influence the reader's interpretation of all the other characters and events in the novel. By the use of this device, Rebecca West is able to give a viewpoint, without it necessarily appearing to be her own. As Chris's cousin, Jenny has known him longer than anyone else. Her memories of their childhood are happy, filled with Chris's innate belief in goodness and faith in his future. Her infatuation with Chris is clear from the start: she wants him to be happy; she finds no fault in any of his words or actions; her appreciation of his physical qualities is that of an observant, dedicated admirer.

Jenny's role at Baldry Court is that of companion to Kitty, although it would seem that she has always lived there. Her love for the house and its surroundings stems from her childhood, but it appears that she would be just as happy to live anywhere, provided Chris was there too. She admires the beauty and perfection which Kitty has created, but she finds in it a certain air of falseness which compares unfavourably with the Baldry Court of her youth.

The reader gets the impression that Jenny's existence during Chris's absence has been mundane. Her days seem to have been filled with ensuring that the house and grounds remain as beautiful as ever, in preparation for his eventual homecoming. She finds her solace in thoughts of his happiness, although her own life seems devoid of any real fulfillment or purpose. Her concern for him also manifests itself in her dreams, which have become a frighteningly realistic depiction of Chris in No Man's Land.

Her initial reaction to Margaret is similar to Kitty's, although, once she senses Margaret's genuine distress, she becomes more sympathetic and her thoughts turn to Chris and his condition. Her attitude to Kitty changes from this moment onwards. She realises that Margaret is concerned only with Chris, while Kitty's selfish nature now seems shallow and unreasonable. When Jenny visits Margaret's home, she adopts a snobbish attitude, which reflects her upbringing and those with whom she now spends most of her time. This is quickly broken down, however, as she is more receptive to the goodness of others: she tries to think well of people, to see beyond their outward appearance, to the real person underneath.

As Margaret continues to visit, Jenny learns that appearances can be deceptive. She rapidly comes to appreciate Margaret's goodness and the two women share a deep devotion for Chris. Jenny's feelings are, however, tinged with jealousy - she knows she will never share the same intimacy with Chris that Margaret does.

Neither of them wants him to be 'cured' - in Jenny's case this is because she just wants him to be safe. Even if their lives are never the same again; even if he returns to Margaret and is lost to her forever, that will be fine, just as long as he is happy and well.

Eventually, Jenny realises that to keep Chris locked in his artificial world would be as cruel as releasing him. He would be mocked and pitied; to see him thus humbled would be devastating. Jenny accepts that the 'cure' is necessary but still resents Kitty's selfish attitude. During the interview with Dr Anderson, Jenny comes to understand that Kitty has always despised her and probably resents her presence, but tolerates her during her husband's absence. There is no love between these two women, as their could have been between Jenny and Margaret under different circumstances.

4. MARGARET

The initial description of Margaret, as given by Jenny, shows her as a woman who is undoubtedly past her prime. However, it should be remembered that this unpromising view is tinged by Jenny's prejudices against people of a lower class than her own. It could, therefore, be argued that this description says more about Kitty and Jenny than it does about their visitor. Margaret is embarrassed about her former relationship with Chris, although this is not because she feels she has anything of which to be ashamed, but because she feels it is improper to discuss this sensitive subject with his wife.

As Margaret begins to describe Chris's illness, she finds Kitty's unfeeling and harsh attitude difficult to accept. Margaret's sole concern is for Chris - and that she should 'do the right thing'. Chris is ill and Margaret feels compassionate towards Kitty, as his wife, because she knows how she would feel in the same situation. She obviously feels uneasy in the grand surroundings of Baldry Court and Kitty's cold reception and rudeness reinforce this sensation. Margaret senses that Jenny shares her concern for Chris, so she pleads with her to rectify the situation. She is worried, with some justification, that Kitty will believe that she and Chris are still lovers, so refuses to show his letter to her, and repeats that they have not met for fifteen years, playing down his importance to her, in order to spare Kitty's feelings. This demonstrates her kind and sympathetic nature.

Margaret seems to have a belief in the goodness of others. She comes to Baldry Court expecting to be able to help; we learn that when she first entered service, she was abandoned by the family for whom she was working, yet she hardly has a bad word for them. She is a cheerful woman, full of compassion and pity: her husband has not made a great success of his life, yet she remains resolutely loyal to him. She desperately wants to help Chris by seeing him again, but she is concerned that her presence at Baldry Court might upset Kitty.

When she first visits Chris, rather than looking upon his house in awe, she pities the amount of work and time he must have committed to its maintenance. This demonstrates her practical nature, which also shows in her treatment of Chris. She does not attempt to hide the truth from him: she explains the situation at their first meeting. Margaret is an honest woman, who does not hide anything which she feels may be of importance, or helpful to Chris. During the interview with Dr Anderson, she reveals details about her relationship with Chris, which the others find shocking. Although she seems embarrassed, she understands that the doctor needs to know the truth if he is going to be able to help Chris.

The discovery that Chris had a child and that this child died at the same age and time as her own son, has a deep emotional impact on Margaret. She makes this discovery in Jenny's room, when she sees the photograph of Oliver on the dressing table. She becomes very upset, both for his loss and for her own, but also because she now knows how to bring Chris back to reality.

The 'curing' of Chris is a matter which puts Margaret in a quandary. She knows how to cure him and feels that, for Kitty's sake, she should help, yet to do so will mean Chris must return to the Army and be placed in danger. Margaret and Jenny share a common desire to keep Chris safe, yet eventually Margaret decides to tell him about his son. This shows her integrity: it would have been easier and less painful for her to say nothing to him about Oliver, but she knows that he cannot be allowed to live a lie. She understands his nature well enough to know that, in his right mind, such an existence would be intolerable to Chris. The cost to them both is immense - they will never meet again. If he survives the war, he will return to Kitty - he is too honourable to do anything else.

Margaret is also a proud woman. This is not the artificial pride of Kitty, whose self-satisfaction, which borders on conceit, stems from her appearance, possessions and status. Margaret has more dignity, which given her background, surprises Jenny. Her self-respect shows her to be a survivor and where lesser women, like Kitty, might falter, she triumphs. She knows that she will have to sacrifice her own happiness in order to 'cure' Chris, but she does this without elevating her own role to that of his saviour. Instead, she regards herself as merely the messenger and she does her duty.

THEMES

1. LOVE

This is one of the main themes of *The Return of the Soldier*, which is, in essence a story about the love of three women for one man. Jenny is obviously in love with Chris, but hers in an unrequited affection, which will never reach fruition. She seems to have accepted this situation and is content to remain in his presence - or at least in his house and be of use to him. Rebecca West demonstrates an element of self-sacrifice in this sort of love: Jenny will never be really happy without Chris, but by remaining where there is no hope of a satisfying relationship with him, she will always be the onlooker and never the recipient of affection. This knowledge has not escaped Jenny, as she points out herself that she is more than capable of feeling self-pity, which implies that she may have reflected on her situation in an unsatisfactory light. Jenny's blind devotion to Chris is so strong and consuming that she is always prepared to put his needs ahead of her own and remain in this disappointing position, dedicating herself to his happiness alone.

Kitty's feelings towards Chris are more selfish. Whether or not there was ever any great affection between them is unclear. When Jenny first mentions Kitty's arrival in Chris's life, it is as someone who merely added to his financial burdens. The reader gets the impression that as Chris was handsome, rich and of good breeding, while Kitty was beautiful and demonstrated excellent taste, their marriage was inevitable. There is no mention of love or passion, Kitty just seems to have appeared on the scene as a suitable wife for Chris. She does not seem to be unduly disturbed by her husband's absence, which demonstrates that their marriage may not have been as happy as she would like everyone else to believe. In trying to 'cure' Chris, at no time does she mention loving him: it is not for his wellbeing that she is concerned, but for her own future. It is ironic that, of the three women, she probably loves Chris the least and yet, eventually, she achieves her desire and gets him back. This situation helps to reinforce another theme of the novel: that those who appear to have everything they could want are not necessarily happy; that there is more to life than appearances and possessions.

Margaret's love for Chris is that intense, once-in-a-lifetime attachment which neither of them has managed to achieve since. The end of their relationship, through his jealousy, seems to have marked the end of her hopes. From that moment until she meets with him again at Baldry Court, her life has become one of drudgery and unacknowledged dissatisfaction. The effect of their meeting at Baldry Court is to demonstrate to all of them how important this emotion is. In discovering the 'real' Chris, Kitty and, more particularly, Jenny realise how false their lives with him had been. He is such a different person when Margaret is with him that he becomes almost unrecognisable to Jenny, who had previously believed her knowledge of his character to be infallible. Of course, in giving Chris up, Margaret shows the depth of her love and her greater knowledge and understanding of his character.

In this novel, Rebecca West demonstrates her view of conventional marriage, which especially among the upper classes, was sometimes entered into for the sake of appearances, finances or convenience. At the time of writing *The Return of the Soldier*, the author was having an affair with H G Wells, with whom she had had a son, Anthony, born within hours of the declaration of the First World War. Wells's refusal to leave his wife - although he always provided for Rebecca and their son - necessarily tainted her view of marriage and love. She appears to have a higher opinion of love than of marriage, as she portrays Margaret and even Jenny as happier, more complete people, than Kitty, who supposedly has everything. Yet, interestingly, it is Kitty - the undeserving wife - who wins. Rebecca West portrays real love as consuming and passionate. Through their love for one another, we learn that Margaret and Chris are really better people - they are stronger, happier, more well-rounded characters who flourish and thrive in each other's company. However, ultimately their hopes are dashed as convention is allowed to conquer their love and Chris is forced to return to his unhappy marriage.

2. CLASS STRUCTURE

The study of class differences and condescending, snobbish behaviour is central to this story. Kitty, Jenny and Chris are upper class, while Margaret is portrayed as lower-middle class. She is not impoverished, but her husband is not a professional man; her clothes are worn and out-of-date, but she does have a servant to help around the house. The difference between Margaret's background and the atmosphere of Baldry Court is personified by Kitty, whose distaste for Margaret immediately becomes clear. What is also apparent is Rebecca West's favouritism of the lower-middle class character. She portrays Margaret as the strong, proud, self-controlled woman, who has much to teach the others; while Kitty - who should be the more powerful character since she not only has money but is married to Chris - is shown as a vacuous, self-indulgent person. Jenny is also shown to have a weaker more dependent nature, which improves through her acquaintance with Margaret.

It would appear, however, that Margaret's awareness of her position in this class structure stems from an earlier experience. When Chris had angrily accused Margaret of behaving inappropriately with Bert, she had assumed that he had done this because he had supposed that, being lower class, she would be less trustworthy than women of his own social standing. The argument that followed marked the end of their relationship.

When she first visits Baldry Court, Margaret is acutely aware of her own appearance and status, but she is most concerned for Chris, and overcomes her feelings of inferiority. Kitty's attitude makes an already awkward situation much worse. She triumphs over Margaret's lowly status, but in doing so, reveals herself as an unattractive, unsympathetic character. In trying to take the moral high-ground, Kitty continues, throughout the story, to reinforce the view that she is a shallow and, despite appearances, rather unlovely representative of her class.

As it transpires, of course, Chris himself does not feel any sense of superiority over Margaret. Any class distinction means nothing to him, compared to their love. Unlike his wife, he does not seem to even notice Margaret's appearance, but views her as the one person who can make his life complete again.

Class distinction also features in the conversation between the three women and Dr Anderson. The doctor speaks to Kitty in a different manner to that which he employs with Margaret. With Kitty, he quickly learns that he must be conciliatory, must sweeten his comments with compliments. In Margaret, however, he recognises someone with whom he can *really* communicate - she demonstrates a greater understanding of the situation than Kitty and the doctor seems to feel more comfortable talking to her. Kitty is, therefore, once again portrayed as somewhat empty-headed, while Margaret is given the more sensible, and in fact, intellectually superior characteristics.

The reader is convinced of the supremacy of the lower classes, as Margaret's behaviour is so much more favourable than Kitty's Eventually, of course, Kitty's victory demonstrates that, in the author's view, the upper classes are always more likely to achieve their aims than the lower and that they will trample on the feelings and views of those they consider to be beneath them. This is a reflection of the changing class-structure during the First World War. Through their service in the war, the working classes ultimately became stronger and more organised, with more definite ideas about their deserved position in society, while for the upper classes, the way of life which they had enjoyed in Edwardian England would eventually become a thing of the past.

3. LOSS AND GRIEF

Various aspects of loss and grief are touched upon during the course of the novel as we see how some of the characters deal with death. Among these are the reactions of Margaret, Chris and Kitty to the loss of their children. Margaret, being a strong, self-sufficient woman, is able to talk to Jenny about the death of her son, Dick. She speaks lovingly of him, remembering the simple pleasures of his short life. The reader comes to believe that she had thoroughly enjoyed motherhood and that, through it, she found a new and more satisfying meaning to her life. The loss of her son has obviously had a deep and lasting effect on her and she seems to blame herself for his death. She asserts that she believes he died because she had little to give him. She is, however, forced to reconsider this assumption when she learns that Oliver, who seemed to have everything, was also taken from his parents.

When she learns of Oliver's death, Margaret grieves openly, just as though the child had been known to her. She senses the injustice that these two infants should have died before their lives had really begun. The reader could draw a parallel here between the deaths of these children, and the deaths of so many young men on the battlefields. The soldiers could also be said to be ignorant of the real cause of their deaths, and with so many dying so young, their lives could also be said to have been only half-lived.

We may assume that Chris's reaction to Oliver's death was similarly profound. He has insisted that the day-nursery be kept, almost as a shrine, to his dead son. In addition, Jenny explains that he had found it difficult to live after Oliver's death. It must also be remembered that Margaret brings him back to reality by reminding him of his son - the one link with his real life that he could never truly forget.

In Kitty, however, the reader can perceive a different reaction altogether. Although we are not told how she behaved at the time, it would seem that, five years on, unlike Chris and Margaret, she has been able to move on from her son's death. When the doctor is trying to find a reason for Chris's unhappiness, she neglects to mention Oliver's death. She believes it to be unimportant in the current situation - implying that this event no longer affects her. Jenny describes the cold look on Kitty's face when she remembers her child, but attributes this to her general reaction to death, rather than a specific memory of Oliver. Interestingly, Margaret first comes across a photograph of Oliver in Jenny's bedroom, rather than anywhere else in the house, which implies that Kitty does not want there to be any reminders of unhappiness in her perfectly manufactured world. Chris's insistence on the maintenance of the day-nursery also irritates Kitty - she can see no point in it. This may be because to have the room kept in this way serves as an unhappy reminder. This conclusion seems unlikely, however, since she could easily avoid entering the room at all, yet always chooses to sit in there after she has had her hair washed. Ironically, had Kitty got her own way, and removed all traces of their child, her means of 'curing' Chris would also have vanished.

It could be argued that in these portrayals of different reactions to death, Rebecca West is providing a comparison between the complacency of some at home during the war, whose lives remained detached and unaffected by events, and the suffering of others whose loss of a loved one would have a lasting impact on their lives. Margaret and Chris represent the latter group, while Kitty personifies those whose arrogance clouded their outlook on all matters other than those which directly affected their own existence.

During the course of the novel, Jenny is also grieving for the loss of her old way of life and her assumed intimacy and understanding of Chris, which she finds to be as false as all the other aspects of her life. She learns that it is not she and Kitty to whom Chris turns for comfort, but to a stranger, whose knowledge of Chris, despite an absence of fifteen years, is superior to that of his devoted cousin.

4. TRUTH AND GOODNESS

Truth and goodness are qualities which are brought to life in Margaret. It is through her inordinately good and kind nature that Jenny learns the value of soul (or self) over beauty. Jenny and Kitty have lived what they consider to be good lives, although of how much value their existences are is debatable. By comparison, they believe, Margaret has lived a fairly squalid life, of little or no importance.

Jenny's lesson comes in the form of witnessing the effects of Margaret's goodness on Chris's personality. It also becomes clear that Margaret is almost incapable of committing a mean act. She shows such generosity of spirit towards Kitty, who has demonstrated nothing but contempt for her. This has a humbling effect on Jenny who, under Kitty's influence, had always placed great importance on appearances and the beauty of her surroundings. Initially, upon Chris's return, she reminds him that Kitty had been everything he could have wished for in a wife. However, the reader can interpret a change in this stance as Jenny becomes more familiar with Margaret. She begins to crave the company of Chris and Margaret, rather than Kitty. She also acknowledges the impact which Margaret's intervention has had on her own life - she no longer has nightmares about Chris wandering through a death-ridden No Man's Land.

By a mutual, yet unspoken agreement, Margaret and Jenny seem to decide that Chris should not be 'cured'. He is happy and safe where he is - to bring him back can only be to his detriment. However, it is their equally silent acknowledgement that the truth matters, that eventually persuades them both that the dreaded 'cure' must be carried out.

Of course, the truth within this story is, that despite Kitty's protests to the contrary, Chris cannot have been happy with his life before the war. He had made the conscious decision not to give his correct address to the War Office and he had done this before the onset of his amnesia. This demonstrates his desperate need to escape from the reality of his life. Jenny's description of him as he crosses the lawn, following his 'cure' reinforces this - he is not a man who has rediscovered happiness. Having found a better place to live and more worthy people to live with, he is snatched away and brought back into his old unsatisfactory world. Goodness has been left behind, and he must learn to live with the truth.

Comparisons

The Return of the Soldier, being a home-front novel, with little focus on the realities of the war from a soldier's perspective has fewer obvious comparisons to be made with much of the other literature of the First World War. However, there are still many areas of the story which can be studied in this section. This is not supposed to be a definitive list of the aspects of this novel which can be compared or contrasted with other works of literature - it is meant to give students a guide or a starting point from which to begin forming their own ideas.

1. HOME-FRONT ATTITUDES

The complacency of those at home is one subject which is admirably portrayed in this novel. Kitty and Jenny are seen to be living an idyllic lifestyle at Baldry Court, their lives carrying on much as before and they seem relatively untouched by the war. It is the spring of 1916 yet they still have a household maintained by domestic servants; neither of them appears to do anything towards the war effort and they regard their sole purpose in life as maintaining the house and grounds in readiness for Chris's return.

This complacent home-front attitude greatly angered some soldiers and poets who were serving at the front and this is demonstrated in many other works of literature. A good example of a poem which covered this subject would be *Glory of Women* by Siegfried Sassoon. In this piece, Sassoon angrily berates women who glorify the war. It could almost have been directed and someone like Kitty, whose serene world seems to have been frozen in the golden days of 1914, untouched by the horrors which have caused her husband's illness. This poem speaks of women who prefer their men to be heroes or wounded (but only somewhere which does not cause embarrassment). This reflects Kitty's attitude to Chris's illness - she seems ashamed that he may have suffered mentally and be unable to recover without medical assistance. In addition, her misplaced confidence that she would have heard if he was injured typifies this complacency and the attitude that nothing should be allowed to overshadow what was once such a comfortable and unspoiled existence. It also demonstrates Kitty's disillusion and refusal to accept the realities of the war and her unhappy marriage.

Criticism of this self-satisfied, complacent attitude can also be seen in some of the works of E. A. Mackintosh, particularly in his poem entitled *Recruiting*. Here he depicts those sitting safely at home as smug and arrogant, happily sending others away to war, while portraying the soldiers who serve as worthy and honourable - the best of men.

In *Birdsong* by Sebastian Faulks, there is another example of this attitude. In one episode, Michael Weir goes home on leave to find that life there remains essentially unchanged. His parents' lives appear to have carried on as before, and it seems to Weir that they now inhabit a completely different world which seems unfamiliar to him. His father is portrayed as an arrogant man, not really interested in hearing of Michael's experiences because he gets all the information he needs from the newspaper reports. When Weir returns to the front, he has developed a deep hatred for those safe at home, which demonstrates a side to his personality which the reader has not seen before.

Strange Meeting by Susan Hill also contains a reference to this home-front complacency and a soldier's reaction to it. At the beginning of this story, John Hilliard is at home, convalescing, having been wounded at the front. He feels so uncomfortable here that he is unable to sleep. His mother, Constance (a character very similar to Kitty), continually reminds him of his duty to the family and the need to maintain appearances. John returns to the front and it is only once he is on the boat and crossing the channel that he can really relax and finally go to sleep. He feels that now he is going home.

A different perspective on home-front attitudes is provided in Erich Maria Remarque's *All Quiet on the Western Front*. When Paul Bäumer goes home on leave, he is surprised by how out-of-place he feels. No-one seems to understand him anymore, but he knows this is because he has changed. Their lives have remained the same, but his experiences have broken him and he can no longer see things in the same way as them. He desperately wants to shield his sick mother from the realities of the war, and refuses to allow his father to show him off in his uniform to all his friends. When the time comes for him to leave again, he is devastated and wishes that he had never returned home - the contrast between home and the war is too great.

The difference between these examples and *The Return of the Soldier* is the perspective from which they were written. Sassoon, Mackintosh and Remarque all had first-hand experience of the war and the attitudes of those at home, and their writing reflects their interpretation of these events. Sebastian Faulks and Susan Hill, on the other hand, were writing in the latter half of the twentieth century. Their stories reflect realistic portrayals of the attitude of serving soldiers towards their own families, who failed to really understand what the war was like. Rebecca West, who wrote her novel in 1918, is less obvious in her portrayal of home-front complacency. Chris is not seen to be angry or bitter towards Kitty; no-one seems surprised by her reaction to the war. To a certain extent this makes Kitty's attitude even more intolerable: she refuses absolutely to allow the war to intrude upon her life - everything *must* remain as it was before, regardless of the cost to others.

2. CHANGED LIVES AND CLASS DIFFERENCES

Another aspect of the war which is covered in *The Return of the Soldier* is the changes which the war brought to the lives of those who lived through it. Rebecca West implies throughout her novel that, for Kitty, a greater impact than the effects of the war would be the loss of her status, which is threatened by Chris's illness. All the plans she and Jenny have made for the future and Chris's return will mean nothing if he cannot be 'cured'. While Kitty struggles desperately to cling on to her old way of life, Jenny's world is already undergoing great upheavals. Regardless of what happens to Chris, her life is shattered. If he remains in his 'old' world, he will belong to Margaret and Jenny realises that she will see less of him and that their relationship will be altered as he will no longer need her. If they 'cure' him and bring him back to reality, he will have to go back to the war and may be killed.

Many home-front authors and poets portrayed this sense that, for them, life was changing: such changes were out of their control and were forced upon them by altering circumstances. For some these changes would be brought about by the loss of a loved-one and a perfect example of this is Vera Brittain, who lost her fiancé, brother and two very close friends during the course of the First World War. The book *Letters From a Lost Generation* chronicles these losses and demonstrates the gradual wearing down of a strong spirit under the weight of so much despair.

Other poets of the First World War also appreciated that the war would bring about an end to their old way of life. Among these was May Wedderburn Cannan, whose life was devastated by the loss of her fiancé in the influenza epidemic which swept through Europe at the end of the war. Together they had planned their future but this was snatched away from them. This sense of desolation and emptiness, typified by the character of Jenny in *The Return of the Soldier*, is reflected in May Wedderburn Cannan's poem *Lamplight*, which was, in fact, written in December 1916. This prophetic poem tells of broken dreams and lives shattered by the death of a soldier whose plans for a happy future will now come to nothing. Her poem *Love 1916* also reflects this sentiment: nothing is as it was; even love has changed - it no longer exists in its old form and has been renamed sacrifice.

This sense of life never being the same again, as portrayed in poetry and fiction of the First World War, reflects a realistic set of trends which was taking place during that time. The First World War would bring about emotional, economic and social changes for many different sectors of society. Some, like Kitty, seemed to believe that they were above such changes and that their lives should be able to carry on as before, little appreciating that no-one was immune to the effects of the war.

There were also far-reaching consequences in the class-system which had dominated in England for so many years. Kitty's haughty attitude to Margaret stems mainly from her belief that those of a lower social status, must be inferior to her own class. The author portrays her as less concerned that Chris may have once been Margaret's lover, and more worried that he could ever have loved anyone who was so plain and dowdy. Today, this snobbery seems harsh and judgemental, but this was not an uncommon attitude at that time. Another example of it can be seen in *Strange Meeting* by Susan Hill. John Hilliard's mother, Constance, openly criticises the station-master for not maintaining the platform very well. She shows distaste for the fact that he has allowed his standards to slip, while mentioning, only in passing, to John that the station-master's son has been killed in action. The characters of Kitty and Constance are valuable to the modern-day reader because they represent the 'old order'. Their type would still exist after the war, but this time marked the beginning of a downward trend in their role and standing in English Society.

Many people who had previously been able to command respect, either because of their status or their wealth, found that as a result of the war, they were no longer in such exalted positions. An excellent example of this can be seen in Remarque's *All Quiet on the Western Front* and this also demonstrates that these changes in society were not uniquely English. Prior to the war, the young men now serving at the front had been at school and their lives had been dominated by an overbearing teacher named Kantorek. He had bullied the young men into enlisting, telling them that it was their duty to serve their country. Eventually, Kantorek is also called upon to do his duty and finds himself in training as a territorial under the command of one of his former pupils. This young man, Mittelstaedt, makes his former schoolmaster's life a misery, but when Kantorek reports this to a senior officer, no-one takes him seriously - he no longer commands their respect: the war has made them equal.

Other authors who use the pre-war class system in their works include Pat Barker in *Regeneration*. Billy Prior, a working-class officer, has a mother whose sole purpose in life seems to have been to see her son rise up the social ladder. This has caused him great difficulties as now he feels that he does not fit in anywhere and results in him feeling equally uncomfortable with both his fellow officers and the ranks. He develops a cynical, resentful attitude, showing disrespect for almost everyone with whom he comes into contact. Pat Barker makes great use of language to portray these class differences. Scenes which relate to Billy Prior, whether they be about his trench experiences, or his sexual preferences, use coarse, down-to-earth language, while conversations between Dr Rivers and Siegfried Sassoon, are always more refined and there is a greater sense of decorum. The irony here is that the topics of conversation between Rivers and Sassoon are usually similar to those between the doctor and Billy Prior, but through the use of language, the reader becomes aware of Sassoon's upper-class status, and Billy's socially inferior standing. As his treatment progresses, Billy is seen to calm down and become less vocally antagonistic which helps to demonstrate that he now 'fits in' better.

Margaret's character in *The Return of the Soldier*, represents the working classes, but unlike Billy Prior, she has nothing to learn from the upper classes. Throughout the novel, she demonstrates a better sense of decorum and generosity than her hostess.

3. CHOICES

In *The Return of the Soldier*, the three women have differing views on whether Chris should be 'cured'. Kitty is desperate that her husband should return to her, although her motives for this are questionable. Jenny initially wants Chris back too: she longs for a resumption of their old way of life and cannot bear the idea that Chris may be lost to her - although, of course, he was never really hers in the first place. As she becomes better acquainted with Margaret and witnesses the joy of which Chris is capable when in her company, Jenny's view begins to change. She starts to doubt the necessity of 'curing' him when he is so happy - and safe. Margaret fears a 'cure' because she knows that this will mean Chris will have to return to the army and the war. She also knows that a 'cure' will not increase his happiness: it will just make him more ordinary. Dr Anderson, while interested in solving the case before him, sees no need to rush towards the 'cure'. Like Dr Rivers in Pat Barker's *Regeneration*, he is possibly in a quandary over the moral integrity of making a man mentally fit again, just to have him sent back to the front and the experiences which made him unwell in the first place. Dr Anderson seems to believe that a delay in 'curing' Chris would cause no hardship. He and Margaret both know that Chris can be cured, and how to do it. They are, however, less convinced of the need for urgency. It is Kitty's forceful, selfish nature, plus Margaret and Jenny's acceptance that Chris would want to know the truth, which eventually enable them to make their choice.

In *Regeneration*, Dr Rivers faces this same quandary every day, particularly in his dealings with Siegfried Sassoon. He understands that it is his perceived duty to make his patients well again, but in doing so, especially in Sassoon's case, he begins to doubt the validity of his role in the war. Pat Barker demonstrates that the eventual physical and emotional cost to Rivers is too great, as he undergoes a breakdown himself.

4. EFFECTS OF WAR ON THE INDIVIDUAL

The effect of warfare on the individual is also a topic worthy of examination. In *The Return of the Soldier*, we are not informed exactly what it is that has caused Chris's amnesia. This, together with his other memories from the past fifteen years, has been erased. This sort of psychological reaction to trauma is also featured in *Regeneration* by Pat Barker. Of necessity, all of the patients featured in this novel, set at Craiglockhart War Hospital, are suffering from some sort of physical or emotional breakdown. The only exception to this could be said to be Siegfried Sassoon, although his dreams and hallucinations demonstrate that his mind is far from settled. These breakdowns have taken on many different forms: Prior has become mute; Burns vomits whenever he is near food; Anderson has a morbid fear of the sight of blood. Dr River's method of treatment is to encourage these men to talk about their experiences and face their fears. Although this is not always successful, in the majority of his cases, as depicted in *Regeneration*, Dr Rivers achieves his costly aim, and his patients are discharged.

The effects on an individual are not always shown in such an obvious or dramatic way. In *Journey's End*, a play by R C Sherriff, each of the men reacts differently to the war. Sherriff had served in the trenches and his portrayal of the characters in his play demonstrates his first-hand knowledge of the varied reactions to trench-life and warfare.

Stanhope, the main character, is close to a breakdown: he continues to function, although his nerves are obviously shattered and he consumes vast amounts of alcohol which seems to dull his senses enough for him to carry out his duties. He is aware of his condition and seems ashamed, fearing that his family might find out and think less of him. Raleigh, on the other hand, is new to the trenches and, therefore, his reactions are based more upon his shock at the change in his old schoolfriend, Stanhope, than on any experience of the war. After the raid, when Osborne has been killed, Raleigh becomes confused by how he is supposed to react, and this leads to a heated argument with Stanhope. Osborne is the most mature character in the play. He is a sensible officer, who appreciates the impact that continuous and sustained pressure of warfare has had on those around him. His is the voice of reason and sense and he has a realistic perspective of the war. Trotter is often seen as a fairly one-dimensional character, but to judge him in this way is to do him an injustice. There are hidden depths to Trotter, which are all the more interesting in that they remain unspoken. Stanhope claims to feel envious of Trotter's ability to retain a sense of normality. Trotter hints that this is far from the case which implies that he has taken a conscious decision *not* to show how the war affects him. His reactions and feelings are locked away, behind the jovial exterior. Hibbert's reaction is different again, in that his sole concern seems to be self-preservation and he continually tries to shirk his responsibilities. Mason's response to the war is perhaps the most interesting of all since he does not appear to have one. He is not an officer, but acts as servant in the officer's dugout, carrying out their orders and worrying over the simple things which directly affect him in his duties. He demonstrates great loyalty to those with whom he serves. At the end of the play, he makes sandwiches for the officers, before collecting his gun and going up into the trenches to face the German attack; just as though this was an ordinary day and he was going to work.

By way of contrast, the main character in *Birdsong*, Stephen Wraysford is initially portrayed as unaffected by his experiences in the war. He is remote and emotionally cut-off from the horrendous scenes unfolding before him. This is due to his reaction to the ending of his relationship with Isabelle Azaire. This self-imposed isolation ends with the death of his friend, Michael Weir and this episode marks a growing awareness within Stephen of his capacity to care for his fellow man. The reader later learns that, at the end of the war, Stephen did not speak for two years: his mental anguish obviously giving him a great need to assimilate his experiences and make sense of them, before he could begin to communicate again.

FURTHER READING RECOMMENDATIONS FOR STUDENTS

Students are often expected to demonstrate a sound knowledge of the texts which they are studying and also to enhance this knowledge with extensive reading of other books within this genre. I have provided on the following pages a list of books, poetry, plays and non-fiction which, in my opinion, provide a good basic understanding of this topic. In addition, a small review of each book has been provided to help students choose which of the following are most suitable for them.

NOVELS

STRANGE MEETING by Susan Hill

Strange Meeting is a beautiful and moving book. It is the story of two young men, who meet in the worst circumstances, yet manage to overcome their surroundings and form a deep and lasting friendship. They are opposites: John Hilliard is quiet and reserved, while David Barton is outgoing and friendly. Despite their differences, their friendship blossoms, as the world around them disintegrates into self-destruction. Susan Hill writes so evocatively that the reader is automatically drawn into the lives of these men: the sights, sounds and even smells which they witness are brought to life. This is a book about war and its effects; it is also a story of love, both conventional and 'forbidden'; of human relationships of every variety. This is a tale told during the worst of times, about the best of men and is, quite simply, one of the best novels ever written about the First World War.

BIRDSONG by Sebastian Faulks

Written in 1993, this novel tells the story of Stephen Wraysford, his destructive pre-war love-affair, his war experiences and, through the eyes of his grand-daughter, the effects of the war on his personality and his generation. A central theme to this story is man's ability to overcome adversity: to rise above his circumstances and survive - no matter what is thrown in his path. Many readers find the first part of this novel difficult to get through, but it is worth persevering. The pre-war section of the novel is essential in the understanding of Stephen Wraysford's character and his reactions to the events which happen later. Faulks's descriptions of battle scenes are among the best in this genre. In our view, this novel is suitable only for A-Level students, due to some adult themes.

A VERY LONG ENGAGEMENT by Sebastien Japrisot

A story of enduring love, truth and determination. Refusing to believe that her fiancé can possibly have left her forever, Mathilde decides to search for Manech whom she has been told is missing, presumed dead. She learns from a first-hand witness, that he may not have died, so she sets out on a voyage of discovery - learning not just about his fate, but also a great deal about herself and human nature. Mathilde herself has to overcome her own personal fears and hardships and, out of sheer persistence and a refusal to accept the obvious, she eventually discovers the truth. Although this novel does not form part of the main syllabus reading list, it does make an interesting and fairly easy read and is useful from the perspective that it gives a French woman's viewpoint of the war.

REGENERATION by Pat Barker

This book is, as its title implies, a novel about the rebuilding of men following extreme trauma. Billy Prior is a young working-class officer - a 'temporary gentleman' - who finds himself at Craiglockhart Military Hospital in Edinburgh, having been damaged by his experiences on the Western Front. It is the job of Dr W. H. R. Rivers, to 'mend' Prior, and others like him, ready for them to return to the fighting, while wrestling with his own conscience at the same time. Interweaved into this central plot is the meeting, also at Craiglockhart, of poets Siegfried Sassoon and Wilfred Owen, who are both there to receive treatment. This mixture of fact and fiction within a novel has created some controversy, but it is a common feature within this genre and one which Pat Barker handles better than most. This is an immensely useful book - even if not read as part of the Trilogy - as it takes place away from the front lines, showing the reader the deep and long-lasting effects of battle upon men, whose lives would never be the same again. Due to some adult content, we recommend this book for A-Level students only.

ALL QUIET ON THE WESTERN FRONT by Erich Maria Remarque

Written from first-hand experience of life in the trenches, this novel is the moving account of the lives of a group of young German soldiers during the First World War. Remarque had been in the trenches during the later stages of the war and this poignant account of war is a must-read for all those who show an interest in this subject. His descriptions of trench-life and battles are second-to-none and his portrayal of the close friendships forged between the men make this an immensely valuable piece of literature. The fact that this, often shocking, story is told from a German perspective also demonstrates the universal horrors of the war and the sympathy between men of both sides for others enduring the same hardships as themselves.

A LONG LONG WAY by Sebastian Barry

Sebastian Barry's novel tells the a story of Willie Dunne, a young Irish volunteer serving in the trenches of the Western Front. Willie must not only contend with the horrors of the war, but also his own confused feelings regarding the Easter uprising of 1916, and his father's disapproval. Willie's feelings and doubts lead to great upheavals in his life, including personal losses and betrayals by those whom he had believed he could trust. This is an interesting novel about loyalty, war and love, although it does suffer from a degree of historical inaccuracy. In our opinion, due to the adult content of this novel, it is suitable only for A-Level students.

NOT SO QUIET... by Helen Zenna Smith

This novel describes the lives of women working very close to the front line on the Western Front during the First World War, as ambulance drivers. Theirs is a dangerous job, in harsh conditions, with little or no respite. Helen (or Smithy, as she is called by her friends), eventually breaks down under the pressure of the work and returns, briefly, to England. An excellent novel for studying the female perspective, as well as the home front.

POETRY

It is recommended that students read from a wide variety of poets, including female writers. The following anthologies provide good resources for students.

POEMS OF THE FIRST WORLD WAR -
NEVER SUCH INNOCENCE
Edited by Martin Stephen

Probably one of the finest anthologies of First World War poetry currently available. Martin Stephen has collected together some of the best known works by some of the most famous and well-read poets and mixed these with more obscure verses, including many by women and those on the home-front, together with some popular songs both from home and from the front. These have been interspersed with excellent notes which give the reader sufficient information without being too weighty. At the back of the book, there are short biographical notes on many of the poets. This is a fine anthology, suitable both for those who are starting out with their studies, and for the more experienced reader.

LADS: LOVE POETRY OF THE TRENCHES by Martin Taylor

Featuring many lesser-known poets and poems, this anthology approaches the First World War from a different perspective: love. A valuable introduction discusses the emotions of men who, perhaps for the first time, were discovering their own capacity to love their fellow man. This is not an anthology of purely homo-erotic poems, but also features verses by those who had found affection and deep, lasting friendship in the trenches of the First World War.

SCARS UPON MY HEART
Selected by Catherine Reilly

First published in 1981, this anthology is invaluable as it features a collection of poems written exclusively by women on the subject of the First World War. Some of the better known female poets are featured here, such as Vera Brittain and Jessie Pope, but there are also many more writers who are less famous. In addition there are some poets whose work is featured, who are not now renowned for their poetry, but for their works in other areas of literature. Many of the poets included here have minor biographical details featured at the end of the anthology. This book has become the 'standard' for those wishing to study the female contribution to this genre.

UP THE LINE TO DEATH
Edited by Brian Gardner

This anthology, described by its editor Brian Gardner as a 'book about war', is probably, and deservedly, one of the most widely read in this genre. The famous and not-so-famous sit happily together within in these pages of carefully selected poetry. Arranged thematically, these poems provide a poet's-eye-view of the progression of the war, from the initial euphoria and nationalistic pride of John Freeman's 'Happy is England Now' to Sassoon's plea that we should 'never forget'. Useful biographical details and introductions complete this book, which is almost certainly the most useful and important of all the First World War poetry anthologies.

NON-FICTION

UNDERTONES OF WAR by Edmund Blunden

Edmund Blunden's memoir of his experiences in the First World War is a moving, enlightening and occasionally humorous book, demonstrating above all the intense feelings of respect and comradeship which Blunden found in the trenches.

MEMOIRS OF AN INFANTRY OFFICER by Siegfried Sassoon

Following on from *Memoirs of a Fox-hunting Man*, this book is an autobiographical account of Sassoon's life during the First World War. Sassoon has changed the names of the characters and George Sherston (Sassoon) is not a poet. Sassoon became one of the war's most famous poets and this prose account of his war provides useful background information.
(For a list of the fictional characters and their factual counterparts, see Appendix II of *Siegfried Sassoon* by John Stuart Roberts.)

THE GREAT WAR GENERALS ON THE WESTERN FRONT 1914-1918 by Robin Neillands

Like many others before and since, the cover of this book claims that it will dismiss the old myth that the troops who served in the First World War were badly served by their senior officers. Unlike most of the other books, however, this one is balanced and thought-provoking. Of particular interest within this book is the final chapter which provides an assessment of the main protagonists and their role in the conflict.

THE WESTERN FRONT by Richard Holmes

This is one of many history books about the First World War. Dealing specifically with the Western Front, Richard Holmes looks at the creation of the trench warfare system, supplying men and munitions, major battles and living on the front line..

LETTERS FROM A LOST GENERATION (FIRST WORLD WAR LETTERS OF VERA BRITTAIN AND FOUR FRIENDS) Edited by Alan Bishop and Mark Bostridge

A remarkable insight into the changes which the First World War caused to a particular set of individuals. In this instance, Vera Brittain lost four important people in her life (two close friends, her fiancé and her brother). The agony this evoked is demonstrated through letters sent between these five characters, which went on to form the basis of Vera Brittain's autobiography *Testament of Youth*.

1914-1918: VOICES AND IMAGES OF THE GREAT WAR
by Lyn MacDonald

One of the most useful 'unofficial' history books available to those studying the First World War. This book tells the story of the soldiers who fought the war through their letters, diary extracts, newspaper reports, poetry and eye-witness accounts. As with all of Lyn MacDonald's excellent books, *Voices and Images of the Great War* tells its story through the words of the people who were there. The author gives just the right amount of background information of a political and historical nature to keep the reader interested and informed, while leaving the centre-stage to those who really matter... the men themselves.

BIBLIOGRAPHY

THE RETURN OF THE SOLDIER by Rebecca West

STRANGE MEETING by Susan Hill

BIRDSONG by Sebastian Faulks

ALL QUIET ON THE WESTERN FRONT by Erich Maria Remarque

JOURNEY'S END by R C Sherriff

REGENERATION by Pat Barker

SIEGFRIED SASSOON - THE WAR POEMS Edited by Rupert Hart-Davis

UP THE LINE TO DEATH Edited by Brian Gardner

SCARS UPON MY HEART Edited by Catherine Reilly

THE FIRST WORLD WAR by John Keegan

BRITISH CULTURE AND THE FIRST WORLD WAR by George Robb

GREAT WAR LITERATURE STUDY GUIDE TITLES

GREAT WAR LITERATURE STUDY GUIDE E-BOOKS:

NOVELS & PLAYS

All Quiet on the Western Front
Birdsong
Journey's End (A-Level or GCSE)
Regeneration
The Eye in the Door
The Ghost Road
A Long Long Way
The First Casualty
Strange Meeting
The Return of the Soldier
The Accrington Pals
Not About Heroes
Oh What a Lovely War

POET BIOGRAPHIES AND POETRY ANALYSIS:

Herbert Asquith
Harold Begbie
John Peale Bishop
Edmund Blunden
Vera Brittain
Rupert Brooke
Thomas Burke
May Wedderburn Cannan

Margaret Postgate Cole
Alice Corbin
E E Cummings
Nancy Cunard
T S Eliot
Eleanor Farjeon
Gilbert Frankau
Robert Frost
Wilfrid Wilson Gibson
Anna Gordon Keown
Robert Graves
Julian Grenfell
Ivor Gurney
Thomas Hardy
Alan P Herbert
Agnes Grozier Herbertson
W N Hodgson
A E Housman
Geoffrey Anketell Studdert Kennedy
Winifred M Letts
Amy Lowell
E A Mackintosh
John McCrae
Charlotte Mew
Edna St Vincent Millay
Ruth Comfort Mitchell
Harriet Monroe
Edith Nesbit
Robert Nichols
Wilfred Owen
Jessie Pope
Ezra Pound
Florence Ripley Mastin
Isaac Rosenberg
Carl Sandburg
Siegfried Sassoon
Alan Seeger
Charles Hamilton Sorley
Wallace Stevens
Sara Teasdale

Edward Wyndham Tennant
Lesbia Thanet
Edward Thomas
Iris Tree
Katharine Tynan Hinkson
Robert Ernest Vernède
Arthur Graeme West

Please note that e-books are only available direct from our Web site at www.greatwarliterature.co.uk and cannot be purchased through bookshops.

NOTES

NOTES

NOTES

www.ingramcontent.com/pod-product-compliance
Lightning Source LLC
Chambersburg PA
CBHW051709090426
42736CB00013B/2615